WILD THINGS!

Giraffe

on a sleepover

Lisa Regan

ILLUSTRATED BY Kelly Byrne

BLOOMSBURY

LONDON BERLIN NEW YORK SYDNEY

Published 2011 by
Bloomsbury Publishing PLC
49–51 Bedford Square, London, WC1B 3DP

www.bloomsbury.com

ISBN   HB 978-1-4081-4246-2
           PB 978-1-4081-5679-7

This book is produced using paper that is made from wood grown in managed, sustainable forests. It is natural, renewable and recyclable. The logging and manufacturing processes conform to the environmental regulations of the country of origin.

Produced for Bloomsbury Publishing by Calcium. www.calciumcreative.co.uk

Illustrated by Kelly Bryne

Picture acknowledgements: Shutterstock: Anky 23tr, Meunierd 23tl.

Printed in China by Toppan Leefung

Contents

Ring, ring. Wild thing!

If you're WILD about animals, today's your lucky day.

There's a giraffe at the door! You could invite it in...

Giraffes are the tallest animals on the planet. Even their legs are taller than you!

4

Giant!

Look out!

It's not only a giraffe's legs and neck that are long.

A giraffe's tongue is about 50 centimetres long – that's as long as your arm!

Keep your parent's pot plants out of reach!

Mmm!

You will need

lots of visits to the garden centre - to replace all the plants that become lunch!

7

Wee!

There's no nice way to say this – giraffes wee everywhere.

They use the stinky smell to tell other animals to stay away.

8

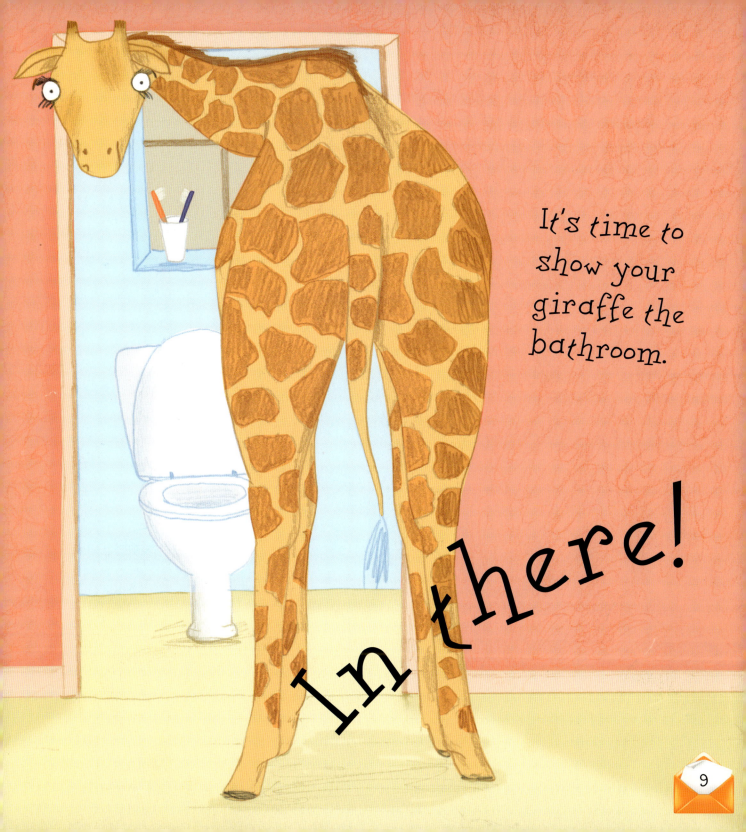

It's time to show your giraffe the bathroom.

In there!

9

Slobber

A giraffe needs a very tough mouth to eat spiky plants.

That makes it dribble a lot. An awful lot.

Munch

Giraffes swallow their food more than once.

They bring large lumps back up their throats and chew them again. This helps them to get more goodness from the leaves.

You will need

leaves and **shoots**

Gulp!

What is THAT?!

13

Yikes!

Watch out for kicking feet – they're huge and they hurt.

A giraffe's **hoof** is the size of a cereal bowl and can kill a lion with one mighty kick.

You will need

slippers for your friend's feet

crash helmet

shin and elbow pads

14

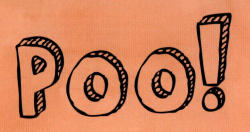

Poo!

Giraffes may be big, but their poo is tiny.

You will need

dustpan

brush

to watch what you eat

16

The neat **pellets** of poo look a lot like grapes or chocolate raisins.

Stop!

Check what you're about to eat...

CHOCO RAISINS

Time to go home

Your giraffe seems happy, but your parents really aren't!

It's time to post your pet back to its real home...

18

A rabbit makes a great pet, but a giraffe is a WILD THING!

19

Cool creatures

A giraffe's neck has the same number of bones as your neck – but they are a lot longer!

A baby giraffe is about two metres tall when it is born. Adults grow up to six metres tall.

Giraffes sometimes fight and use their head and neck to **butt** each other.

Giraffes spend up to ten hours a day eating. Their favourite food is the super-spiky Acacia tree.

Lying down is tricky for giraffes, so they usually sleep standing up.

Giraffes live in Africa. **Herds**, made up of six or seven giraffes, roam the **grassland** looking for food.

Glossary

butt *to hit something with your head*

crash helmet *a hard, round helmet that people such as motorcyclists and racing drivers wear to protect their heads*

grassland *land covered in grass*

herds *groups of plant-eating animals*

hoof *the hard, round part at the end of a giraffe's leg*

karate *a fighting sport in which people kick and punch*

pellets *small animal poos*

shin *the bony part at the front of your lower leg*

shoots *new plants that grow from the soil*

22

Thanks for having me!

The Zoological Society of London (ZSL) is a charity that provides help for animals at home and worldwide. We also run ZSL London Zoo and ZSL Whipsnade Zoo.

By buying this book, you have helped us raise money to continue our work with animals around the world.

Find out more at zsl.org

ZSL
LONDON
ZOO

ZSL
WHIPSNADE
ZOO

Take them all home!

ISBN   HB 978-1-4081-4247-9
        PB 978-1-4081-5678-0

ISBN   HB 978-1-4081-4246-2
        PB 978-1-4081-5679-7

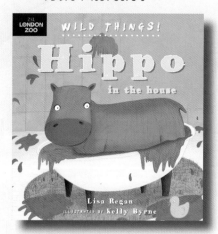

ISBN   HB 978-1-4081-4245-5
        PB 978-1-4081-5680-3

ISBN   HB 978-1-4081-4244-8
        PB 978-1-4081-5681-0